My little desert home

I live in Picture Rocks Arizona, a desert community northwest of Tucson. It's a humble abode, a 1974 single-wide trailer on an acre. A little piece of the Sonoran Desert in a floodplain. As a result, it is lush by desert standards. There are several species of prickly pear and cholla, along with ironwood, palo verde, mesquite, catclaw and hackberry. And with all those plants you get the usual suspects: rabbits, ground squirrels, quail, doves and lizards. I see a lot of desert iguanas. Occasionally I'll see road runners, bobcats and coyotes.

And javelinas.

It was several years before I saw one on my property. Sightings had been very rare over the years, although I would occasionally see hoof prints. One time, a family of them started "camping out" in my yard. I was excited to see them and really wanted them to stick around for awhile. Also wanted to make sure my presence was known. No clue what I was doing. Thought I was being sly when slowly approaching them, but invariably there would be one I didn't see. It would get spooked and run off. After 2 days, they had enough of me and didn't see any again for many years. Their second appearance was brief. After that, a random hoof print or a partially eaten prickly pear, but I never saw them.

I finally saw them again on December 20th, 2020. These are my first photos. Just 2 of the group. I had ordered a new camera and longer lens, though had neither at this time. I was probably over 50 feet away. Photos were taken well after sunset and these are heavily cropped. When they started getting frisky, I left them alone. I knew they had started sleeping under my trailer. Didn't know at the time that the space underneath was to become a place to have babies. They didn't stay there, but would leave the property and return as they saw fit.

I had visited them a few times after the initial contact and they seemed somewhat used to me. Attempting to approaching them was ineffective and yet I could be 3 feet away as they would just walk right by me.

One day, a little more than a month after first contact, I was shooting a cellphone video. It was quite a surprise when about 10 feet away, 2 of them rubbed each other and then started mating right in front of me. Blatant carnal exhibitionism. No shame at all.

Not an expert on critter mating, but I can attest that if you're looking for exhilarating action in animal copulation, javelinas are a major letdown

Here they are, doing what they do best

A group of javelinas is called a squadron. I think of "squadron" as an air force term. Not exactly true, but as javelina are often referred to as pigs, it made me speculate if the old saying, "When pigs fly" had anything to do with the designation.

THEY'RE NOT PIGS, the experts exclaim. They're peccaries, dammit! Collared peccaries in fact. Probably that whole Pangaea breakup thing or something. We don't make bacon out of them but many folks find them tasty. They are pig-like, with their round bodies on little legs, their snouts and hooves. By scientific classification, peccaries and pigs are both of the suborder Suina but different families. New world pigs.

And they stink, as so many people feel compelled to tell me when I start talking about them. Their musk gland smell is very important and they frequently rub each other to maintain a group scent. The squadron can range in size from a few to a dozen or more. The initial group I encountered had 5, although did see a sixth one once. There was definitely a dominant male. They tend to control the harem.

I had installed a skirting around the bottom of my trailer. I never finished it as the last sections involved significantly more work and laziness prevailed. A void waiting to be exploited. The squadron took advantage of this and decided to move in. Could have made efforts to get rid of them but decided not to, even though this meant I was setting myself up for potential repairs.

The opportunity to get intimate photos of the squadron presented itself. I didn't have to go looking for them. My home coincided with their natural range so I had to figure out how to co-exist. The learning process began.

Wildlife photographers are capable of getting shots as least as good as the best ones in this book. But the time, travel, expense, and commitment would be mind-boggling. Photos on these pages were taken on 43 different days. That's a lot of expeditions.

Every one of these photos was taken on my property. I have a large, lets call it "inventory" of "stuff" laying scattered, in piles, or crammed into sheds. The additional 2 non-working 60's Ford Econoline vans cement my trailer trash status.

It was March 2021 when I first saw the 2 babies. The first couple of times I saw them, it was at least an hour after sunset, so it was quite dark. I kept my distance, probably 50 feet away. It's possible that mom didn't want the newborns out when it was lighter. Being so dark and not having a longer lens made it impossible to get any useful photos. At that time, I didn't even think about getting semi-close.

After that, I only saw one baby

3/7/2021

Aw, so cute

These shots above are clips from a video. Didn't dare at the time to get any closer than this, probably 40 feet away. This little guy was still quaking a little. The dark circles under the eyes become less pronounced and the reddish color fades over time. Mom and dad stay together with the newborns when they're this little.   Right photo: going under my trailer.

I shall confess that I have terrible short term memory, which is not improving with age. Made no concerted effort to chronicle the actions of the group. And this memory defect is one reason I didn't even try to identify the individual members. They all look about the same. The dominant male was somewhat more obvious since he was a little larger. Never had the inclination to give them names.

The squadron disappears and then returns 2 months later.   No kid with them.

Perhaps the group were weary of their sightseeing excursions, as they started hanging around more often. Maybe they were starting to like me. Yeah, right. These guys are constantly on the move. Seems likely that survival is paramount to their itinerary.

The first thing one learns about javelinas is that unless you intervene, they will do whatever they please without reservation or apologies.

I've stayed in better places   3/7/2021

Not only do these guys have no qualms about digging up your yard, they will dig up new areas instead of using places they've already disturbed. Sometimes in the same day. I guess they like a change of scenery. Maybe a change of dirt. Or they're just trying to be a nuisance.

Yeah? Well, you don't smell so good either

The rest of the herd generally wanted little to do with me. This is the dominant male staring me down. The big guy was the one who would usually approach me and he was often checking me out. At this time this was as close as he got.

On May 27th, I'm watching the squadron. The big guy starts to approach me. He keeps walking. As I stand there, he comes right up to me and touches my blue jeans with his nose. My first close encounter.

A little later I grab my camera to go visit them. It's a nice day....

Do not disturb

I'm in charge here

I'm coming for you   5/27/2021

With camera in hand, I pay them a second visit. I want to mention 2 things at this point. Javelinas can do serious damage. A few people have even been killed by them. One feature that differentiates peccaries from pigs is their tusks. Their upper and lower canines match together and are self sharpening. However, I never noticed any aggressive behavior from this crew.

The second thing that perhaps needs mentioning is that I often prefer to not wear clothes when outside on my property. With my camera, I sit down sans clothing, at the edge of a little wash. The group is relaxing on the other side. Even though I'm "exposed" I'm not the least bit nervous. Then the big guy gets up and starts walking toward me. Veers left as he crosses the wash. Swings to the right and yawns. He keeps getting closer. I hold my ground.

Then he touches my knee.

When he made contact, I didn't and still don't quite know what to make of it. However, having a wild animal checking me out was not lost on me. An unforgettable moment.

Yeah, you

Closer

CONTACT

Wildlife experts say it is wrong to feed wild animals, as this makes them dependent. I generally agree. I'll confess that I break that rule with my hummingbird feeder. As for other critters, I'll throw out some bird seed for the birds, rabbits and other critters. To avoid dependency, I do it randomly. At least a week or more between feedings. In more urban areas, many people feel compelled to feed javelinas. While a typical weight for an adult male is 40 pounds or so, I recall one report of some "city" javelinas weighing 70 pounds. These become dangerous when they lose their fear of humans. And it is their tendency to cause mayhem, as many people who live in an urban area can attest.

I do give them water. As for food, they ~~pig out~~ help themselves to the bountiful prickly pear plants on my property.

I had a cheap old trunk. I kept a sack of bird seed in there and it didn't take long for the herd to become aware of this. Turns out they love bird seed. I left it unlatched and they would open the lid. I removed the seed sack but there was still an amount of spilled seed on the bottom, so their persistence didn't stop.

The funny thing about this pursuit is that their necks are too short to allow them to reach anywhere near the bottom. This did not discourage them. I then latched it. However, they frequently dig with their noses and bring up roots by lifting up. The latches were not a challenge.

One day, one determined individual was checking out the trunk. I yelled at it and chased it away. My admonition was short lived as it was back about a minute later, trying again. These guys are so obstinate.

What's in there? 6/17/2021

I could have just cleaned out the seed. Decided to put some concrete pavers on the top to weigh it down. Clearly underestimated their determination.

That's when they destroyed the top. While not wanting my trunk ruined, I was impressed by their sheer diligence and strength. And they got nothing for their trouble.   Serves them right.

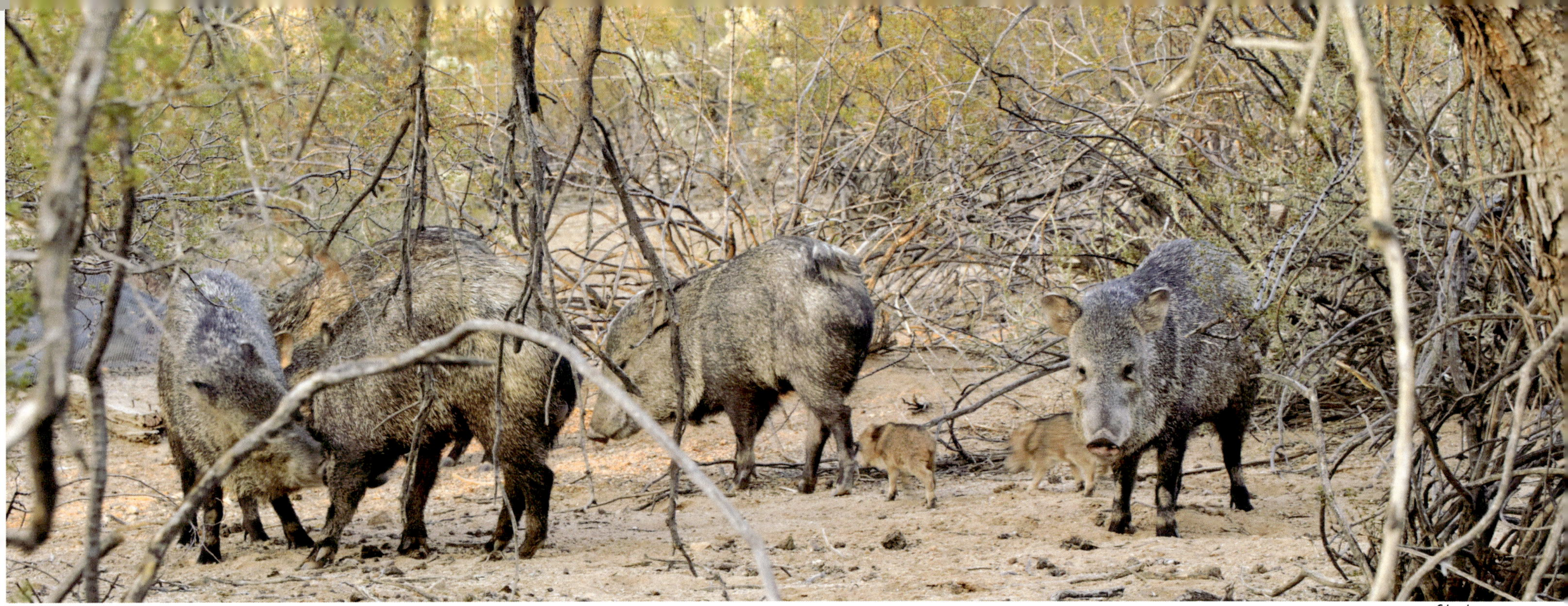

The javelina restroom 6/25/2021

Javelinas pee wherever they want, but they insist on a designated spot when they defecate. Perhaps one with good scenery. Or at least a line of sight for predator vigilance. And they're not like cats or something, although they're capable of scraping with their hooves. I've seen them scrape the dirt *before* they go. What for, I have no clue. They leave their feces on full display. This doesn't make for the prettiest presentation when photographing newborns. This is where mama and the newborns spend most of their time. Where they go.

6/25/2021

The new babies born June 2021

6/26/2021

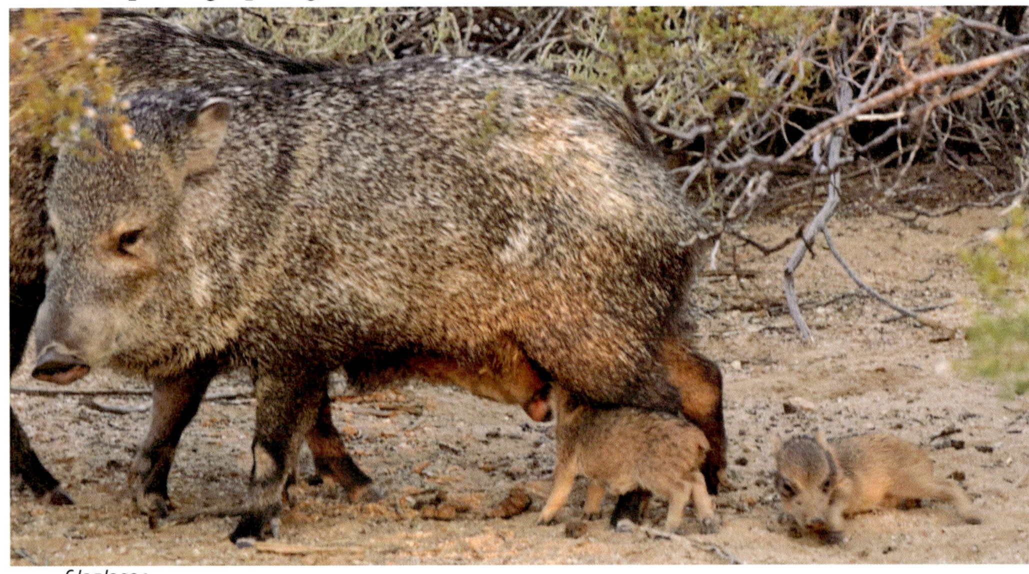

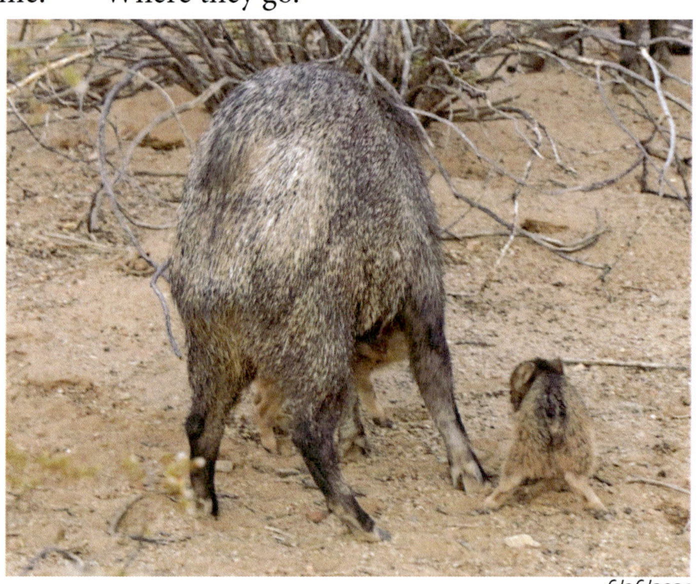

6/26/2021

We're keeping an eye on you

So how do they eat prickly pear? Very carefully. Or not. I still don't get it. I once had this theory that they had an enzyme in their mouths that dissolved the needles. An erroneous speculation. A doctor who had examined their mouths told me that they do have needles in their mouths. I'm guessing that the way they chew tends to break up most of them. I did see one bite off a piece of jumping cholla one day, the nastiest cactus there is. After the piece fell to the ground, the javy stepped on it before eating it, which I suspect was a way to mitigate the intensity of the spines. All I could think of was "ouch".

I have one prickly pear that has very large pads and is about 11 feet tall. One day, a section of it broke off. It was about 4 foot long and I thought, "Great. I can take this piece and transplant it." The javys had their own agenda. It was gone in 2 days.

They're working on finishing it off here.

I did some "research" on these guys via Google. An occasionally dubious resource, but at least a potential step above pure speculation. It cracked me up though, that so many articles mentioned that prickly pear is their favorite food. I doubt it. Fairly confident that if you put down a prickly pear pad and something like an apple, the pad won't be their first choice. Perhaps it's better to classify it as their most reliable desert food source. And it is one way to get water.

Great source of fiber

This was the end of June 2021

The squadron disappeared 2 weeks later as they wandered off to parts unknown. No goodbye, forwarding address, or anything.

6/26/2021

It would be 5 months before
I would see them again

6/30/2021

Stay away from my kids

It's unfortunate that I don't have photographic evidence of the strangest encounter I had with the lead male. But then it would have been quite difficult to capture. It was July 13th, just before they split for 5 months. I usually wear my old shoe "slippers" when outside. The big guy approaches me and clearly finds my left shoe interesting. He does something which looks and feels like he's trying to eat my shoe. I'm taken aback. The rationale of my next move escapes me. I then lifted that foot. He starts to bite down on it.

I wasn't in the mood for my shoe to become his meal, especially since my foot was in it at the time. I take exception to this, so as I deliver a verbal protest and make a threatening move, this javelina honcho decides he's not that hungry and departs.

Two other members of the squadron bear witness and are clearly intrigued. They approach me, apparently to determine what makes my shoes so interesting. Luckily, consuming them was not on their agenda. They merely slobber. This was the only time any other javelinas actually made contact with me.

7/11/2021

7/13/2021

12/3/2021

Back 5 months later.

It's now December 2021. The 2 young'uns look like small adults, along with 2 new babies. A total of 7 in the squadron. I don't actually recall if these 2 babies were born here. I do know these are the first photos of them. What I'm assuming were the previous babies I now classify as "teenagers". I noticed they had a little more hair on the top, almost like a javelina pompadour.

Up until that time none of the others showed much interest in me, but I was about to witness a behavior I hadn't seen previously. One of the "teenagers" would start to approach me. It would get about 12 feet away.

Then with a sudden change of heart, it would quickly run away. Don't know if it was the same one or both of them, but this happened a few times.

12/4/2021

Hi dad

About 10 days after spotting them in December, I only saw one baby

This kid did make it though

Making a puddle

12/18/2021

Their malodorous musk scent is essential for marking herd members and territory. The javelina rub happens frequently. The group shares this scent so that each squadron will have it's own shared "fragrance".

1/16/2022

1/2/2022

Javy heart

It's perhaps lack of olfactory sensitivity, but it became apparent to me that the intensity of the group scent tends to vary significantly. Often I don't really notice it. Other times, they smell rather funky. I'll tell them, "You guys really need a shower".   They just ignore me.

1/16/2022

Now it's 2022. Here is the kid who was making a
puddle a month earlier. They grow up so fast.

1/16/2022

1/16/2022

Does this desert make my butt look big?

So relaxed

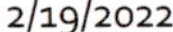

2/19/2022

Deep in contemplation

The scent gland is located about where this one's nose is

When it was daylight, I often wanted to photograph these guys, but they never coordinated their schedule with me, nor did they make any attempt to be accommodating. There were a few days where I would take a bunch of shots, go inside, then come out about an hour or so later and take some more. This day was particularly rewarding. All of the javy shots, from page 20 to the first one on page 26 (where they're leaving for 3 months) were taken on the same day.

Most of the time though, it was after the sun went down. Several of the shots in this book were taken well after sunset.

Yawning is contagious

Sometimes it seems like these guys sleep 23 hours a day. They might spend an entire day underneath my trailer, perhaps coming out once for a potty break. Don't know what they do there but I'm guessing they're not reading books or playing chess. Then they'll come out and maybe walk around for several minutes. Or they might have arrived from elsewhere around sundown. They would then bed down in the yard and sleep . Sometimes, one javelina or a few might get up, locate a new nesting spot and sleep some more.

And yet they still apparently don't get enough sleep, since yawning occurs frequently.

2/19/2022

Note how the little guy is checking me out with his nose

2/19/2022

Aren't I handsome?

2/19/2022

I regret not having photographic evidence of the next behavior. Didn't actually see it.

I never was and still not an expert on javy behavior. A few months after initial contact, I had yet to contemplate what javelinas thought of dogs. Just assumed they would be considered a nuisance, and not a threat like coyotes.

Au contraire.

Sometime in 2021, I found a discarded 2 chambered dog dish. Being the scavenger that I am, grabbed it and thought this would be handy for giving water to the squadron. They came along and drank the water from the dog dish. After drinking the water, they ripped the dog dish apart as you can see in the "reconstruction" photo to the right. Not exactly a surprise considering their proclivity for destroying things.

Here's the weird part. Just destroying it clearly wasn't satisfactory. It's apparent that these dog-scented pieces of plastic needed to be scattered. For several days, I would find pieces of this dish redistributed at various places around my property.

Partial witness to one unfortunate incident

One day the squadron came waltzing onto my property like they owned the place, as they usually did. It was after sundown and saw they had bedded down. Well after dark, they either decided to try a different spot or they were venturing toward the entrance under my trailer. I'm inside the trailer and didn't know this until I heard a horrible racket. Then heard a loud dog yelp. Got up and opened the door in time to see them give chase.

Went out a little later to check on the group. I only saw one individual and it looked freaked out.

I had assumed that the cry of distress I heard was from a dog, since I don't know what a coyote sounds when it's been wounded.

24

2/19/2022

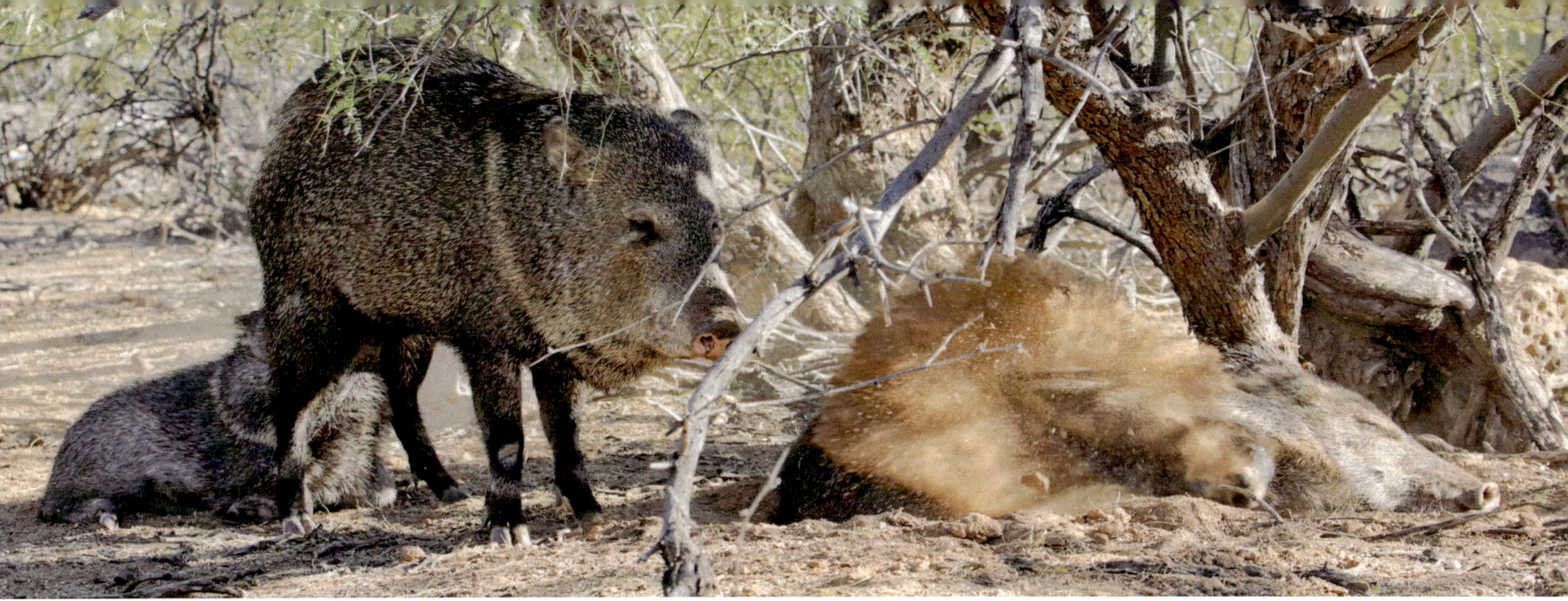

Still nursing at 2 months

That's about when they usually stop

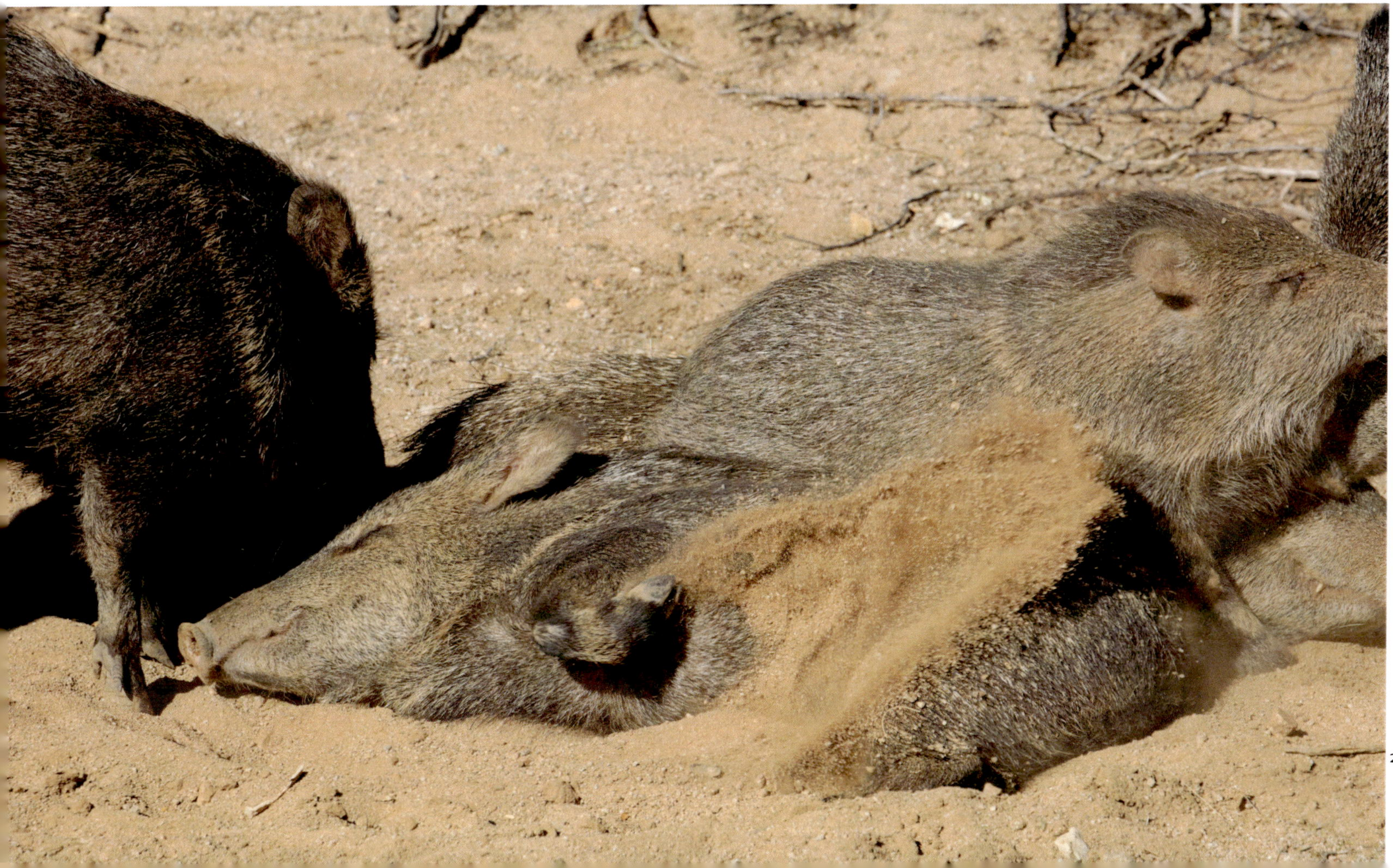

Dust storm

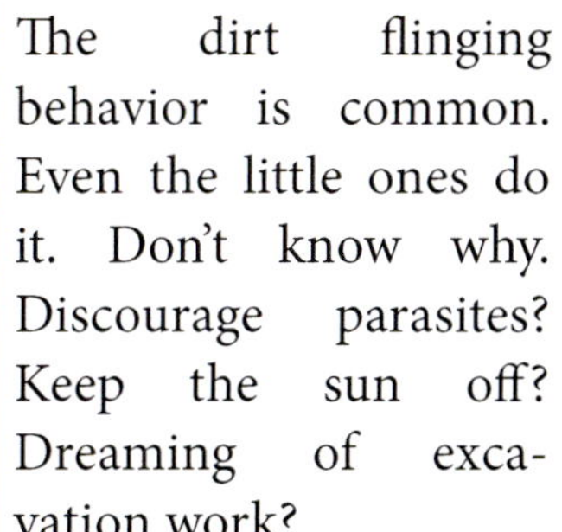

The dirt flinging behavior is common. Even the little ones do it. Don't know why. Discourage parasites? Keep the sun off? Dreaming of excavation work?

It's amusing to watch on the occasions when the others in the line of fire get sprayed with dirt

2/19/2022

2/19/2022

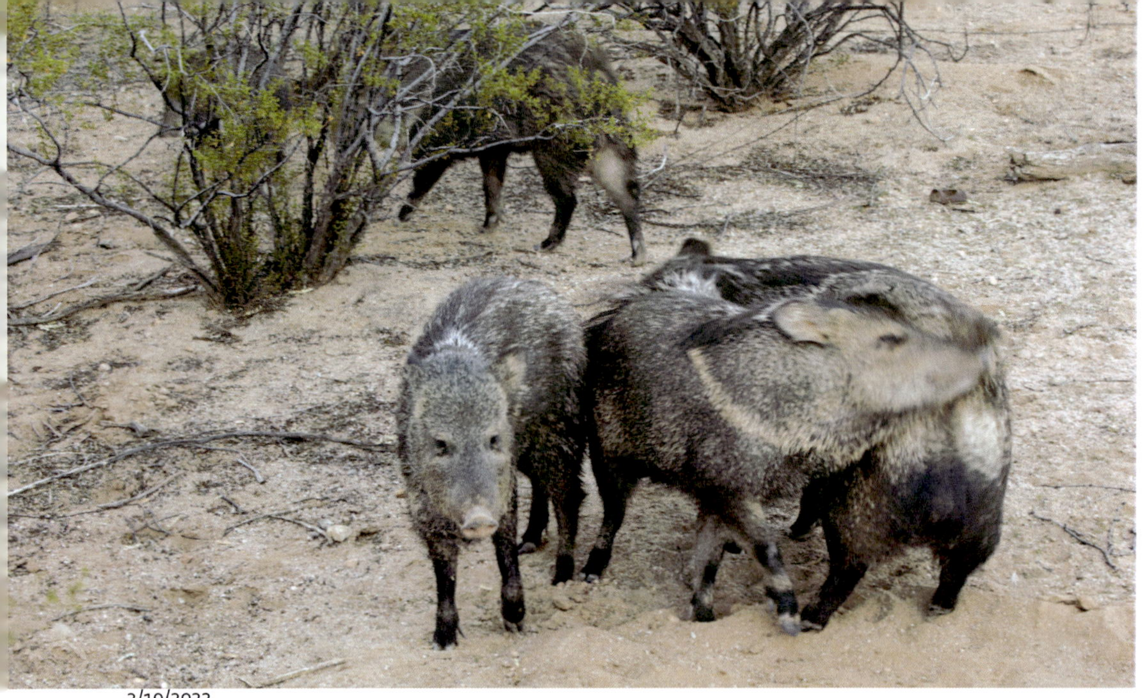

Last look in February as 2 are already sneaking away

One more rub for good luck

Now it's May

A new baby

The other kid is getting big

Three gone. Now only 4 in the squadron including the new kid. The others, either on vacation, moved to Texas or became tacos.

At least I could now tell them apart most of the time. Note that the male above on the right has a cut in his ear and the area above the eye is a little lighter on the female. Same with the older kid.

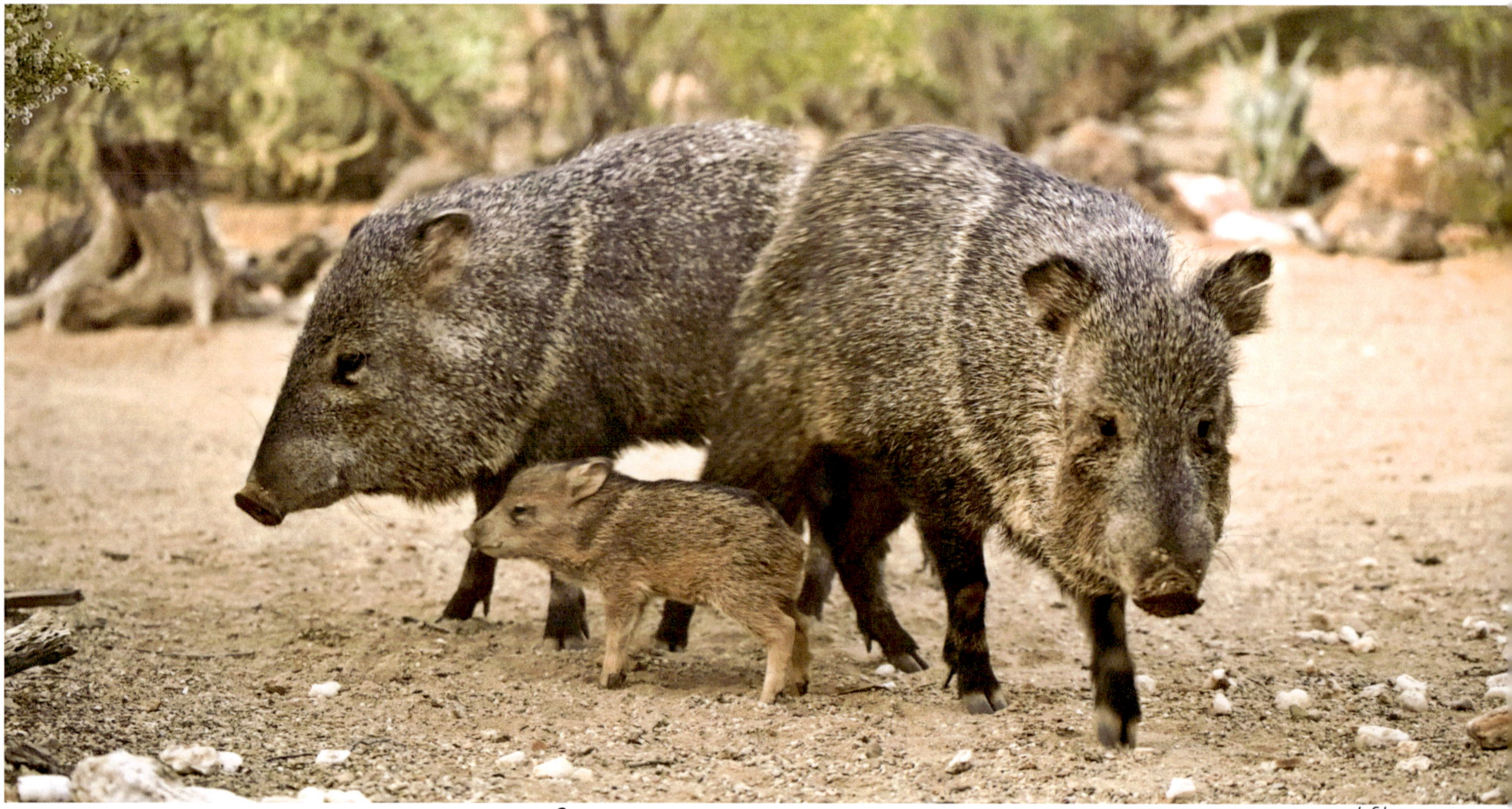

5/16/2022

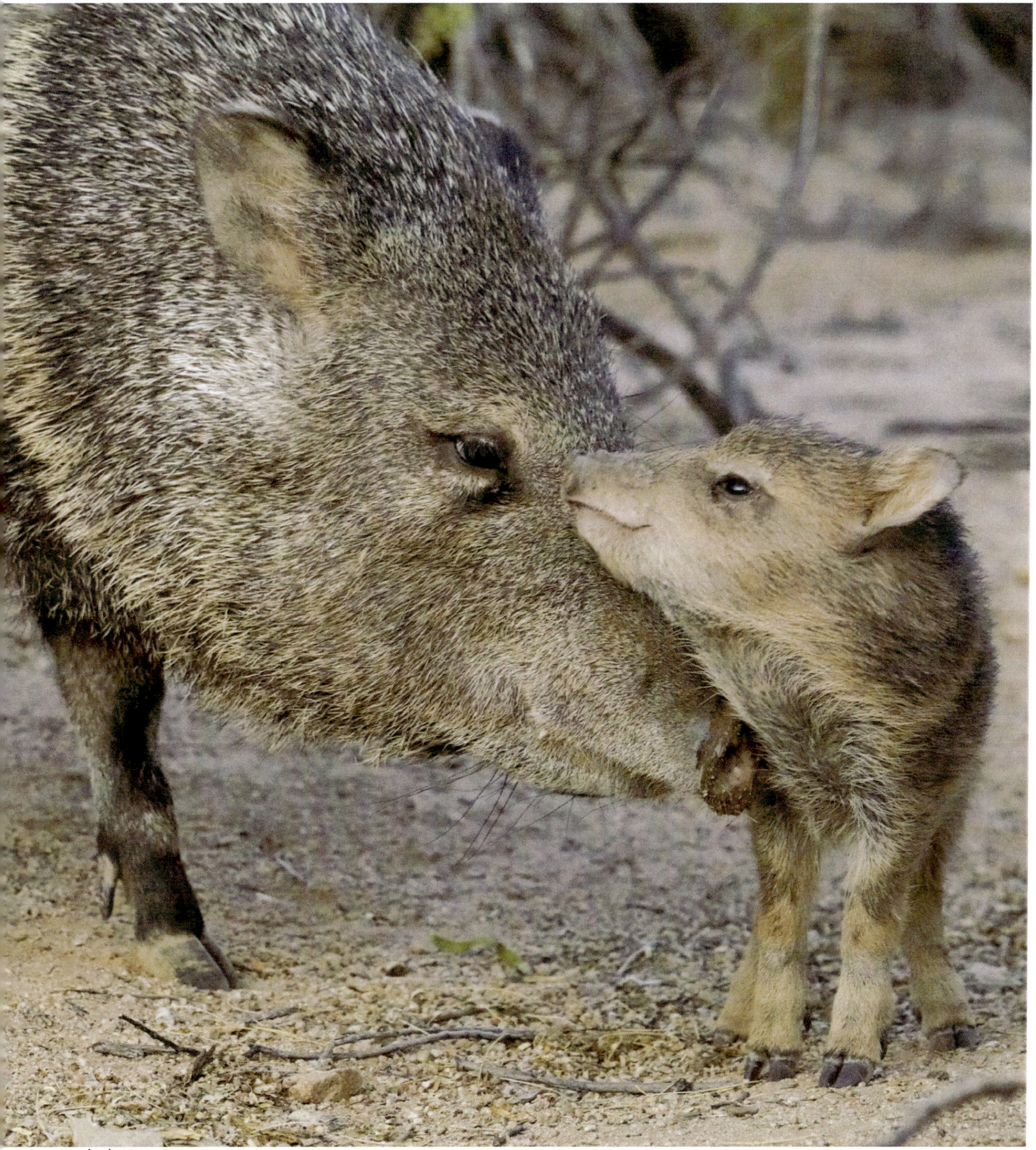

5/23/2022

5/23/2022

6 months old

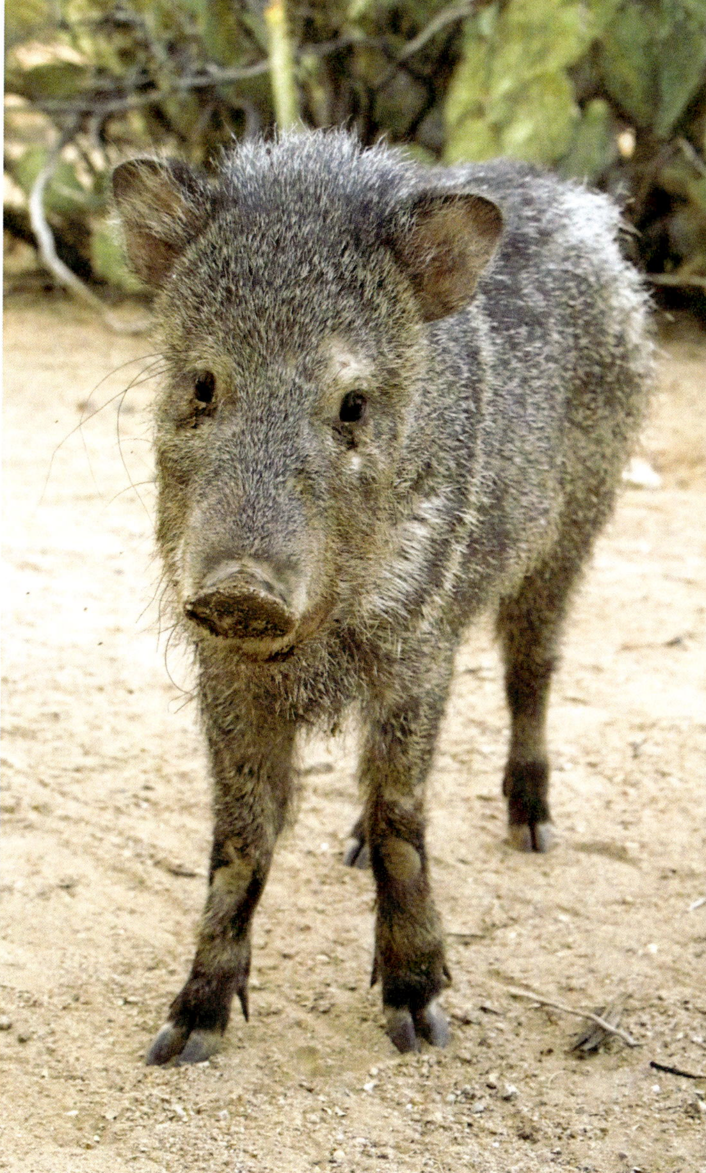

Javelinas are bristly and seem to have a coarse disposition to match. Not exactly a dainty critter.

Nonetheless, it's clear that the familial relationship is close, especially with the little ones. Parents are always checking out the kids.

5/27/2022

6/3/2022

28

Since 2021, it was usually the young'uns that would check me out. This is one of the times the adult male paid a visit.

6/1/2022

6/6/2022

Dad checking out the kid

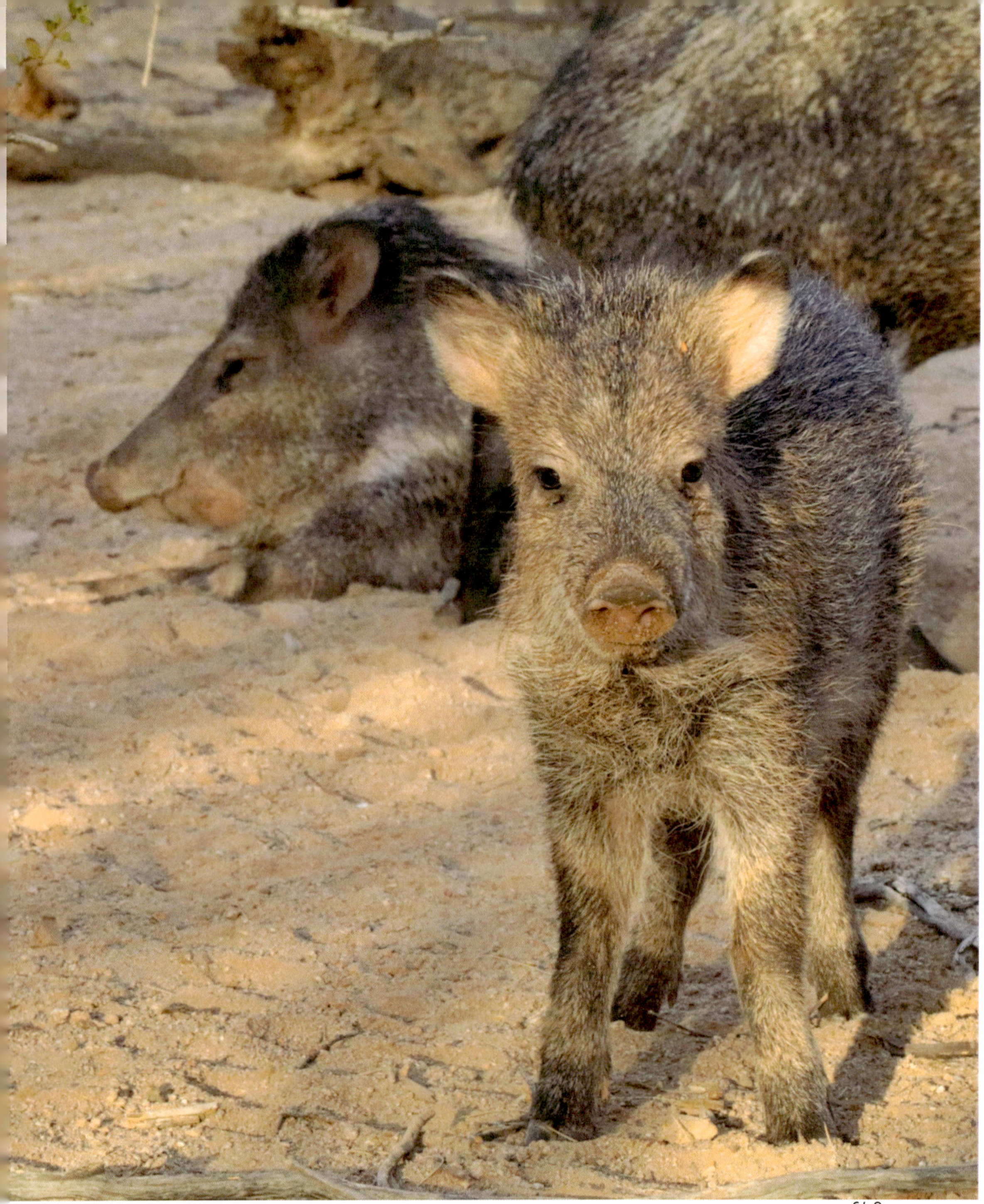

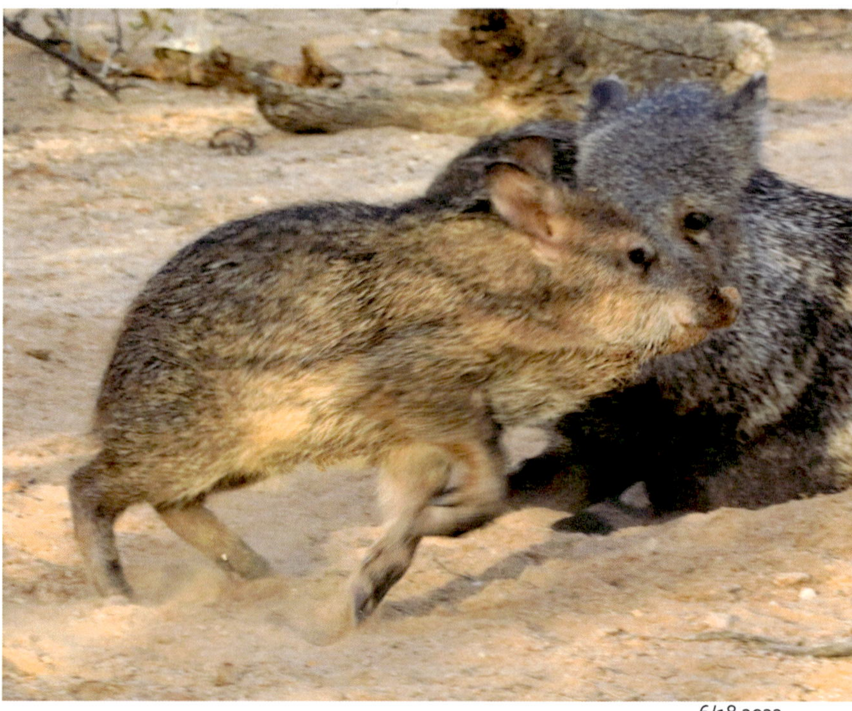

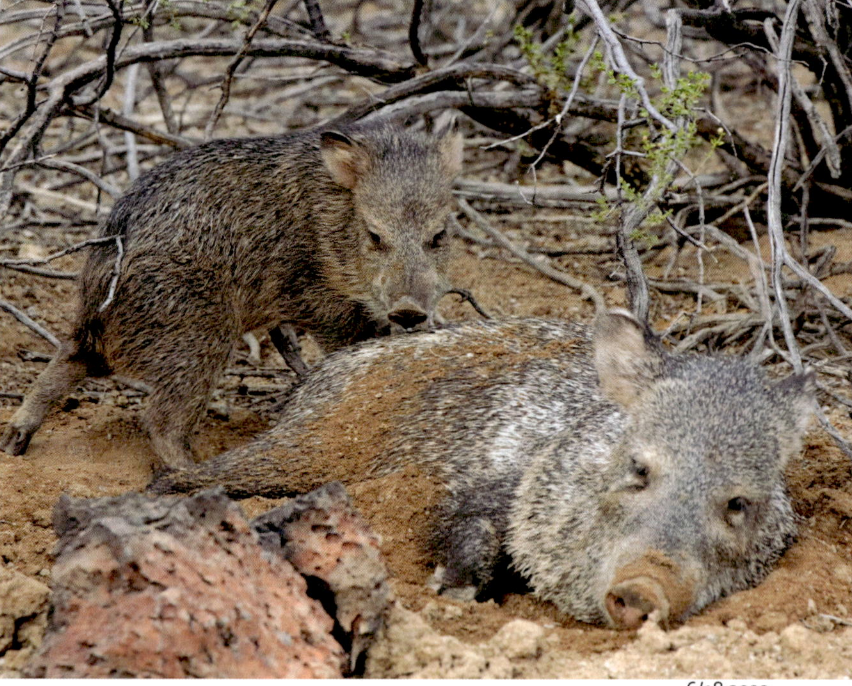

6/18 2022

This little guy was fairly brave. Several times he would slowly approach me, getting about 4 feet away before running off.

6/18 2022

While the adults just want to chill, the youngsters are fidgety and just won't stay put. Just like most little kids.

6/18 2022

Got your snout

6/20/2022

I have a swamp cooler and it has a "bleeder" line to help prevent mineral buildup. Don't want to waste water so I use this line to give a few of my plants some encouragement. As it was summertime, this turned out to be an invitation. Javelinas are unapologetic opportunists and their noses easily find damp ground. Nice cool dirt to lay in.

Didn't want certain plants damaged, so I had to put the water line next to trees instead of the plants I wanted to water. They've got me so trained. Enjoy the damp soil, you thankless peccaries.

6/20/2022

6/20/2022

6/23/2022

6/30/2022 **Mmmm, creosote**

I wasn't going to include this photograph since it might offend some, but I don't want to deny little kids the poop stuff they demand. I need to honor my demographic.

(It doesn't usually look like this)

6/23/2022

32

The young'uns

One day, the older kid starts destroying one of my solar lights, which consisted of a sphere made of plastic balls

Don't know what it was about this globe that motivated the destruction but after totally destroying it, he and the little one started chewing on the little balls

7/6/2022

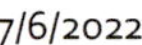

7/6/2022

Here is the squadron the next day at the scene of the crime. They were all chewing on the balls.

7/13/2022

Momma has an itch

7/13/2022

Javelonga

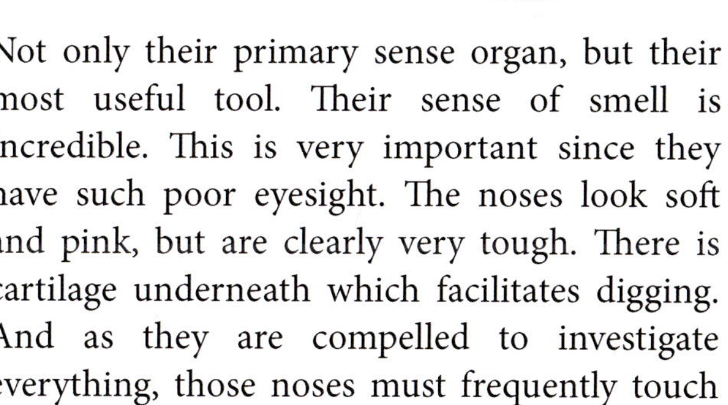

Those amazing noses

Not only their primary sense organ, but their most useful tool. Their sense of smell is incredible. This is very important since they have such poor eyesight. The noses look soft and pink, but are clearly very tough. There is cartilage underneath which facilitates digging. And as they are compelled to investigate everything, those noses must frequently touch cactus needles.

The kids are playing   Going after the legs is common   Probably good practice for when they confront critters like coyotes

The playing looks aggressive, but isn't. However, there are actual squabbles that happen. Out of the blue, a snarl and then it's over as quick as it began. Like a "Hey don't do that" or "Knock it off" protestation. Occasionally a brief tussle. It was never obvious to me what precipitated such actions.

In the summer of 2022 they would stop by, usually after the sun went down. Then take off after a few hours.

They were especially uninteresting during this period, since what I usually saw was 4 javelina sleeping.

This particular day was different. I go out and check on them and happen to see the older kid bothering the little kid. Ran back to the house to grab my camera for a video shoot. I prefer to use a tripod for video but no time for that.

7/13/2022

Now the little one wants to sleep but the older guy has other ideas. This is the only photograph. The older one won't leave the kid alone. The video is on YouTube titled **Javelina Kid Trying To Sleep**.

These are still clips from the video

Like with all critters, the javy babies are the cute ones. The newborns are especially adorable. Like human babies, they are clumsy and totally dependent on mom. But unlike human kids, they are walking the first day. And soon they start to act like grown-up javelinas. I really wanted to watch them grow up. However prior to May 2022, the squadron would disappear soon as the babies were born. Didn't see the 2 that were born July 2021 until 5 months later. Next one born in December resurfaced 2 months later for just a day or 2.

But when this guy came along, the squadron paid several visits after he was born. I took advantage of this and got a lot of good shots of him growing up. Here he's 2 months old.

About a week after this shot, the squadron vanished for 3 months

     Little javelonga   7/15/2022

The kids playing again

Gonna getcha

7/15/2022

Feeding time

Don't know if any individuals ever got hurt during these encounters. I never saw it.

Back off

Two new babies in October

Now the squadron is 6

10/23/2022

10/23/2022

10/23/2022

40

So just how do I interact with them? The primary answer is: Very carefully. They are prey animals with poor eyesight in a hostile world. They are quite skittish. No matter how much time I spent with them, they were never calm. Just a wave of the hand would set them off.

Because of their poor eyesight, I would have to make some kind of noise to approach them. I chose to just vocalize. So every time I went out to see them, I would talk, sing, grunt or whatever, continuously until I got their attention. When I didn't, they weren't shy about protesting my sudden presence. At the very least, their hair rises up some.

When they're really scared, their hair will flare up, exposing the rump area around the scent gland. I saw the fright response from behind once. With the white hair underneath and the pale pink skin, it looked like a flash. Also, they will clatter their teeth when upset. The one in the photo on the right doesn't happen to be scared. Just shaking off dust.

There was one vigilant behavior I witnessed a couple of times. I call it the "freeze". As they're walking along they suddenly stop and just stand there motionless with one front leg in the air. When they get the all-clear (which was never apparent to me), they continue on their way.

A strategy for consuming prickly pear is to break off a section first. It's easier to eat when it's on the ground.

10/31/2022

There's one behavior that still puzzles me. Many have noticed that they will drink water put out for them. Then they will flip the pan, dumping the rest of the water. I've seen a few videos posted that show this behavior. One theory is that they want clean water. That was my first thought, but then I pondered, "like the clean water they get in the wild?" In fact, I recall a time when I would put out a clean full pan and next day the water would be muddy. Made no sense until I saw why one day. The dominant male took a drink, walked over the pan, plopped down on it, got up and continued walking.   Strange.

11/13/2022

After it got tipped over a few times, I tried a big rock and a solid concrete block next to it. Then 2 rocks. Then a rather heavy piece of slag seen here. Now it's the slag with two concrete stakes hammered in the ground and tied together. So far so good.

Is the squadron more used to me now? Absolutely not. If anything, they seemed to tolerate me more in 2021 when the male leader kept an eye on me.

I even have a direct measure of how much time, and to a certain extent when, they are on my property.

The Javelina Restroom. Their current spot, which they've used for about a year and a half, is a passageway on my property which becomes a feces minefield at its worse. It's not too bad now. Rain, dung beetles, and javelina poop thieves have kept the yard in check.

They had a different bathroom when they first started visiting in 2020. Abandoned because of plumbing issues or something.

These guys have their own plans and they're not going to share them with me. I have no clue if they'll come back. I was denied the opportunity to get photos of these young'uns growing up, like I did months earlier. So for now, I say good-bye to these cantankerous critters.

Feeding them turns them into deadbeat welfare recipients. They become gluttonous and lose their fear of humans. This makes them much more dangerous. They are not your friends nor will they ever be. Don't do it.

Also most attacks on humans happen when people are out with their dogs. They really hate dogs. Keep your dogs in check. If you're out walking your desert tortoise or your pet tarantula, you're probably safe.

And if javelinas visit your property, they will show no respect. They will eat those delicious new plants you just planted. They will dig up your yard. They will investigate everything. In their incessant quest, they won't turn down any opportunity, as they knock over your garbage can. For many, these marauding creatures are assholes.   Those pesky pigs!

    No, javelinas are just being themselves   It's their territory   Your garbage can gets turned over because that's their job

    And the young'uns are sure cute

Goodbye   **_Thanks for visiting_**

This was supposed to be a book of photos. Didn't expect so many words infiltrating my visual presentation. I've never had much money, so photography has been a very expensive hobby. About the time these pesky pigs decided to hang out at my place, I had ordered a refurbished version of my dream camera, a Canon 5ds-r. Also, my only lens had been a 24-70 zoom, so I finally purchased a Canon 70-300 lens. This combination were invaluable for the images in this book.

When the javelinas started showing up, I knew right away that I had an opportunity. Had no intention at the time to do a book. This changed when I got careless at a Tucson fair event where I had a booth. While packing up, someone grabbed a bag which contained, among other things, my camera and both lenses. This was a devastating blow, especially since I don't have the funds to replace them. As I had a documentation of their visits over a 2 year period, a book seemed like a viable option. Time to make lemonade. And here it is.

Some photos are clearly better than others ("why is there a hose in the picture?"). Honoring the timeline was important to have continuity and some "lesser" photos were added as a result. I have an abundance of decent photos of these critters. Initially put in so many of what I considered the best, had to take out about 25 of them. There are still over 160 photos in the book.

My main dysfunction is that I tend to do everything myself. I've had no formal training and definitely not a "natural" writer. I've always had to self-edit everything I write. I used to think I was a decent writer. It took several re-examinations over a period of months to get a text I could live with. Still haven't mastered commas. Received some valuable insights from Doug Biggers. Thanks Doug.

There are many "self-publishing" companies that offer their services for neophytes like me. I eschewed these offers, especially the "free' 45 minute consultation that one company offers. So even though I'm a rank amateur, I became editor, proofreader, layout designer and cover designer. Layout design is the one thing I was somewhat comfortable with. My first cover design was terrible, second was a significant improvement and my third attempt will have to do. It was not arrogance or pride so much as poverty which made me reject all offers for professional assistance. I did get proofreading help of my last draft from my brillant daughter, Melissa. While this book has it's flaws, I can live with the imperfections.

I've received flack for the Those Pesky Pigs title. In my opinion, it fits the tone of the book. A friend (who did not give me permission to use her name) suggested it and I adopted it without hesitation. But then, if it looks like a pig, walks like a pig, quacks like a pig then... OK, so peccaries don't quack the same, but the one notable feature that they have in common is the nose. From University of Michigan's Animal Diversity Web: "The snout of peccaries has the same mobile cartilaginous disk and terminal nostrils as pigs." In the 1990's, I worked at the Arizona-Sonora Desert Museum for 4 years. Staff were adamant about informing visitors that javelinas are not pigs. What amused me is that everybody who worked there at the time, especially the critter folk that dealt with them, had no qualms about calling them pigs. Neither do I. But then I've never been a fan of political correctness.

javelinastore.com
Contact: **javelinabook@gmail.com**
Ajo Press © 2023

Those Pesky Pigs update

It's the end of July 2023 as I write this and the squadron has continued to visit. More have disappeared and 2 more babies were born. I mentioned on the last page that it was the theft of my camera and lenses that prompted the creation of this book. Still don't have the better camera but did replace the the 24-70 lens, a steal at about $800. I'm able to continue photographing them, but without the longer lens it's more of a challenge.

My acre, outlined in blue. You'll note a higher density of vegetation. More critter friendly.

As of now, the squadron prevails

5 individuals seeking a living in this hostile desert